INTERNATIONAL ORGANIZATIONS AND LAW

A PROGRAM PAPER OF
THE FORD FOUNDATION

FORD FOUNDATION
NEW YORK, N.Y.

Other papers on Ford Foundation programs:

Too Little, Too Late: Services for Teenage Parents
Child Survival/ Fair Start
Not Working: Unskilled Youth and Displaced Adults
Refugees and Migrants: Problems and Program Responses
Civil Rights, Social Justice, and Black America
Hispanics: Challenges and Opportunities (English and Spanish)
Women, Children, and Poverty in America
The Ford Foundation's Work in Population
Ford Foundation Support for the Arts in the United States
Early Childhood Services: A National Challenge
Work and Family Responsibilities: Achieving a Balance
Affordable Housing: The Years Ahead

Additional copies of this report, as well as a list of other Foundation publications, may be obtained from the Ford Foundation, Office of Communications, 320 East 43 Street, New York, N.Y. 10017.

Library of Congress Cataloging-in-Publication Data

Ford Foundation.
  International organizations and law.
     p.   cm. — (A Program paper of the Ford Foundation)
     ISBN 0-916584-43-7
     1. International agencies—Research.   2. International
cooperation—Research.   3. International law—Research.   4. Ford
Foundation—Research grants.   I. Title.   II. Series.
JX1904.5F67   1990
341.2'072—dc20   90-45175
                                                    CIP

483 September 1990
© 1990   Ford Foundation

CONTENTS

PREFACE

The political changes that swept around the world last year, from the Soviet Union to South Africa and from Central Europe to Latin America, raised hopes for a new era of freedom, peace and security, and respect for human rights. These changes, however, have also contributed to renewed economic rivalries, border disputes, and interethnic tensions. To protect the momentum toward freedom and human rights and also to help resolve whatever conflicts may emerge, there is a continuing need for strong international and regional organizations and international legal arrangements.

In many parts of the world, the growing divisions between the haves and have-nots and the fragility of democracy are threatening economic and political stability and undermining the foundations of the international system. As this paper notes, one of the greatest global challenges today is how to integrate the poorest countries into that system. Large parts of Asia and most countries in Africa and Latin America are having great difficulty adapting to a new industrial age. Instead, they are caught in a downward spiral of debt, economic stagnation, and in many cases political turmoil. These enduring problems of development also call for multilateral responses organized through international institutional and legal mechanisms.

Since no single nation now dominates the international order, international organizations face very different challenges than they did forty years ago in the aftermath of World War II. This paper examines some of those challenges and describes the various ways the Foundation seeks to help citizens, governments, and international institutions recognize the role that international organizations and international law must play in confronting the new realities of global interdependence. After reviewing the Foundation's longstanding interest in strengthening international organizations and international law, the paper describes three areas of future grant making: promoting research and policy analysis; helping institutions improve their capacity to provide research and training in international organizations and law; and encouraging the general public, particularly in the United States, to take a greater interest in international organizations and public international law.

The paper was prepared by Karel Vosskuhler, a program officer in the Foundation's International Affairs program, for presentation to the Foundation's Board of Trustees. It is being published because of the importance of the subject and because of renewed public interest in the potential of international law and organizations like the United Nations to help resolve not only conflicts between nations but also such common problems as dangers to the environment, refugee flows, terrorism, interethnic violence, and violations of human rights. In that way, international organizations and international law can be powerful forces for advancing world peace and prosperity.

Franklin A. Thomas
President
Ford Foundation

HISTORICAL
PERSPECTIVE

Although the first half of the twentieth century was dominated by two world wars between powerful nation states, the second half has seen an increase in international cooperation, a gradual diffusion of power away from the two superpowers, and the growing importance of non-state actors in the international system.

Each major war in modern history has been followed by an attempt to secure future international peace and security, with each successive effort involving a larger number of nations. After the Napoleonic wars, a few great powers assembled at the Congress of Vienna in 1815. For the rest of the nineteenth century they maintained a relatively stable balance of power through the "Concert of Europe." The Hague Peace Conferences of 1899 and 1907 were the culmination of the nineteenth-century peace movement. The first brought together delegates from twenty-six nations to promote the peaceful regulation of international conduct. The second conference, which followed the Russo-Japanese war of 1904–05, was attended by delegations from forty-four of the fifty-six nations that claimed sovereignty at the time. After World War I, the League of Nations embodied an even more ambitious attempt at securing international peace and security, but in the 1930s the league fell apart when new aggressor-nations terminated their membership—Nazi Germany and Japan in 1933, Italy in 1937, and the Soviet Union in 1939.

Early in World War II, the Allies began considering the creation of a new world organization. President Franklin D. Roosevelt initially foresaw a postwar order in which each of the four great powers—the United States of America, Great Britain, the Soviet Union, and China (France came in later)—would assume far-reaching responsibilities for conditions in their own regions, on the basis of a mutual recognition of spheres of influence. In November 1943 Roosevelt, Winston Churchill, and Joseph Stalin met in Teheran to discuss these ideas further, and during subsequent negotiations at Dumbarton Oaks in Washington, D.C., it was decided that the new organization would have a General Assembly with universal membership and a Security Council that would be dominated by the great powers. After the United States, Great Britain, and the Soviet Union had resolved some outstanding issues at the Yalta Conference in the Crimea, representatives from fifty countries assembled in San Francisco in February 1945 to negotiate the Charter of the United Nations. The Statute on the International Court of Justice, established earlier at The Hague, became an integral part of the U.N. Charter.

The United States also played the dominant role in the creation of the postwar economic system, embodied in the institutions established at a conference in Bretton Woods, N.H., in 1944: the International Monetary Fund (IMF) and the International Bank for Reconstruction and Development (IBRD), or World Bank. Due to opposition in the U.S. Congress, the International Trade Organization (ITO) never came into being. The General Agreement on Tariffs and Trade (GATT) covers only part of the mandate of ITO. Although not an international organization, GATT has developed into a substitute mechanism for international trade liberalization.

The international system of institutions has undergone dramatic changes from the model envisaged in 1945. The membership of the U.N. has more than tripled and the tasks of the U.N. and its specialized agencies have expanded. Early on, the U.N.'s mandate to maintain international peace and security was frustrated by disagreement between East and West, which caused a deadlock in the Security Council. But U.N. peacekeeping, which had not been foreseen in the U.N. Charter, became a major endeavor. The important role played by the U.N. in support of the decolonization process is now almost completed. U.N. involvement in technical and economic assistance to developing countries has grown. The U.N. also came to play an important role in promoting international awareness of human rights and other global issues. In general, the demands on international agencies and their leaders continue to increase and to change.

NEW   CHALLENGES
IN   A   CHANGING
INTERNATIONAL   SYSTEM

On December 10, 1988, U.N. Secretary General Javier Pérez de Cuéllar accepted the 1988 Nobel Peace Prize on behalf of the U.N.'s peacekeeping forces. In his acceptance speech he said: "The prospects of realizing the vision expressed in the Charter of the United Nations seem better today than at any time since the organization was founded." Indeed, the East-West climate has greatly improved and there are indications that the superpowers prefer to reduce their involvement in regional conflicts and make greater use of U.N. mechanisms to help solve them. For the first time since 1945, the permanent members of the Security Council are working closely together on a number of issues, and the Secretary General is playing a more active role than has been possible for many years.

But going back to 1945 will not be good enough to meet the needs of the world we live in. The international system has undergone dramatic change since World War II. For one thing, with the emergence of Japan and the Federal Republic of Germany, the number of influential powers has increased. For another, such non-state actors as transnational corporations and nongovernmental organizations (NGOs) have assumed increasing importance. Governments have a hard time keeping up with the pace of change triggered by the technological and information revolutions. Differences in various nations' abilities to adjust to rapidly changing circumstances is widening the gap between rich and poor nations. And new global problems, such as environmental degradation and climate change pose both immediate and long-range dangers.

It has become a cliché to say that, in an age of global interdependence, international cooperation has become imperative for all nations. In the Soviet Union, President Mikhail Gorbachev seems to have concluded that his country can only hope to maintain its great-power status by adjusting to current international realities and by sharing in the technological revolution that has created global markets for products and capital. Gorbachev and his close associates have made a host of suggestions for a more active U.N. involvement in the resolution of international conflicts, and they make frequent references to the importance of respect for international law in the conduct of international relations.

The new winds blowing from Moscow have improved the international climate. They are having a favorable effect upon arms control negotiations between East and West, are leading to some extent to superpower disengagement from regional conflicts, and seem to offer better prospects for economic cooperation between East and West. The new era of detente puts a premium on economic rather than military power.

In the face of Gorbachev's diplomatic initiatives, one could easily lose sight of the success of Western economic, political, and military cooperation over the past forty years, in particular through the North Atlantic Treaty Organization, the European Community, and the summit meetings of the seven leading industrialized countries (Canada, France, the Federal Republic of Germany, Great Britain, Italy, Japan, and the United States). In the past decade, most Western nations have successfully carried out domestic economic and social adjustments, and made progress in coordinating international policies. They now find themselves in a good position to reap maximum benefit from the postindustrial revolution, which is profoundly affecting the international division of labor.

The greatest uncertainty, and the greatest challenge, in the evolution of the international system concerns the integration into the system of the developing countries in the southern part of the globe, which are often referred to as the "Third World" or the "South." In view of the growing differences in stages of development between various groups of developing countries, some consider it inappropriate to continue to use such aggregate descriptions. This notwithstanding, the gap between the "haves" and the "have-nots," both between and within countries, continues to grow, compounded by growing imbalances in demographic and technological trends. A few East Asian nations are successfully making the transition to a new industrial age, but most countries in Africa and Latin America and large parts of Asia are having great difficulty adapting economically and politically. Instead, they remain caught in a downward spiral of indebtedness and economic stagnation.

Problems of underdevelopment tend to intensify as they accumulate. Rampant population growth erodes the physical resource base, which in turn causes a flight from the countryside, leading to a concentration in the cities of the unemployed, most of them young and many of them educated. They form a potential vanguard for revolutionary action and a source of recruits for criminal and terrorist groups. Without minimum prospects for economic improvement, many countries, ranging from truly poor ones like Bangladesh to formerly rich ones like Argentina, have little hope for democracy and stable governance. These conditions are unlikely to produce governments that will be able to play constructive roles in the international system. The threat of political instability in many developing countries becomes even more serious in light of the continuing militarization of their economies, the proliferation of sophisticated weapon systems in highly unstable regions, and the dispersal of such weapons among terrorist and other criminal organizations.

What does this imply for international organizations and international law? First of all, it is abundantly clear that no single nation now dominates our age. The United States, the architect of the postwar order, is no longer able to control events singlehandedly, if it ever could. Japan, the European Community, the newly industrializing countries (NICs), and the dominant nations in some regions have become influential international actors. The Soviet Union, the East-Central European nations, and other developing countries are likely to become more involved over time. Partly as a consequence of this diffusion of power, international organizations face far different challenges now than they did forty years ago. The United Nations, the Bretton Woods institutions, and the international trade system are all under strain. With the increase in the number of players, decision making has become more complex. It is not clear how or by whom leadership will be exerted in years to come. Adjusting to the new realities of global interdependence will remain a challenging process for citizens, governments, and international institutions alike.

This paper explores the implications of the changing international environment for the Foundation's grant making in the field of international organizations and law. The paper first discusses problems associated with international cooperation and multilateralism. After a brief review of the Foundation's previous involvement in this field, the paper describes three areas of future grant making: research and policy analysis; capacity building; and educating the general public and encouraging interest in the field.

PROBLEMS OF
INTERNATIONAL
COOPERATION

Lack of Consensus

One may agree that interdependence dictates cooperation, but the kinds of cooperation possible are subject to the preferences of the countries involved, all of which have different interests and values. Even with largely successful cooperation among Western nations, "new thinking" in Moscow, reform in East-Central Europe, attempts at structural adjustment in many developing countries, and a more businesslike climate in the United Nations, no consensus exists about the purposes and directions of international cooperation.

Unfortunately, the globalization of markets, the technological and information revolutions, and the emergence of certain global threats to resources and the environment do not, in themselves, turn a world of nation states into a global community. The image of the global village, developed in the early 1970s from such diverse sources as satellite pictures of the Earth, the celebration of Earth Day, and Marshall McLuhan's writings, does not easily translate into global policies. If one thing is clear by now, it is that, given the realities of demography and resource availability, Western modes of development and Western life styles cannot be extended to all of the world's citizens without causing irreparable damage to the planet.

The Western model exerts growing attraction, but expectations of following it seem likely to be disappointed. It is difficult to foresee what will happen once larger societal forces in the South, in and out of government, begin to recognize the durable nature of the North-South rift and the risks implicit in many Western models. It is even harder to assess the implications for international cooperation. The difficulty of simply applying Western models may lead the developing world to a gradual shift in emphasis from global to regional and sub-regional cooperation.

Some would cite various global problems—such as the depletion of the ozone layer, the greenhouse effect, and the pollution of the air, the seas, and other "global commons"—as incentives for worldwide cooperation. Finding consensus solutions to these problems, however, will be far from easy. What is now often called "sustainable development" is interpreted in different ways in different parts of the world, reflecting differences in demography and technological development. Depletion of domestic resources is a far more serious problem in the South than in the North, where information-intensive technologies are, in many instances, reducing the demand for such resources. On the other hand, energy consumption in the North still accounts for a larger part of global warming than does the destruction of the forests in the South.

Under the circumstances, bargaining on these issues between North and South promises to be extremely contentious. Southern governments, increasingly beleaguered by frustrated electorates and rebellious youth, will have very little incentive to make concessions to the North, though some nations may occasionally settle for such mutually beneficial arrangements as protection of the environment in exchange for reduction in foreign debt. In many cases, "sustainable development," though in the best long-term interest of the countries involved, will not be in the best short-term interest of their governments. For these reasons, a global public interest—requiring global management and package-deals between the North and the South—will emerge only very gradually, if at all. Research can make a contribution here, devising innovative legal and economic arrangements through which the international community might compensate developing societies for opportunities forgone by acting to protect the global environment.

In the South, the rationale for international cooperation seems, in many cases, to be quite weak. This is clearly illustrated by the example of the debt crisis. So far, cooperation in this field has not led to equality of burden sharing, but rather has exacted the heaviest toll from some of the world's poorest people. Basic asymmetries in interests between North and South will continue to frustrate mutual accommodation in other areas, like that of the liberalization of trade in goods and services, the protection of intellectual property rights, and the outlawing of chemical weapons. In many instances, the North has a much larger stake in promoting international order than the South, in terms of both political and economic security. Governments of certain developing countries may be tempted to exploit to maximum advantage the leverage deriving from this particular asymmetry. They may justify such action by the exploitation they have endured at the hands of the powerful North. Here, again, the challenge is to come up with new mechanisms that may facilitate sensible compromises.

In the North, one may also expect mixed feelings about interdependence. International institutions are no longer under the full control of Western nations. Rather, they represent the often perplexing diversity in values and interests throughout the world. Nor will a more diverse international system necessarily be stabler than the present one, which has long been dominated by a few great Northern powers. The world may well be heading for an era in which international tensions derive less from enmity between the great powers than from social disintegration within weaker nations. Already, the cases of Lebanon and Uganda are no longer unique, with countries like Peru, Sri Lanka, and Cambodia also displaying dangerous levels of domestic turmoil. For citizens in the prosperous North, this lack of order will be very difficult to understand.

International organizations and international law will have to operate in this highly unstable environment for the foreseeable future. In many instances, they themselves will be highly controversial, as was the U.N. during the past decade. The South, and the dispossessed generally, will continue to see them as possible instruments for change. The North, however, is likely to stress their support of the status quo or their ability to afford protection against disorder and disintegration in various countries and regions.

In sum, it is important to realize how profoundly the lack of consensus affects the possibilities for global cooperation. But this is a challenge as well. Research and debate can elicit new ideas that may help bridge the North-South divide and provide incentives for institutional cooperation and constructive international law.

Lack of Understanding

Linking the fields of international organizations and international law to multilateral cooperation in itself reflects certain articles of faith, both intellectually and in policy terms. It suggests an underlying conviction that institutionalized global cooperation is a necessity, despite the problems noted above. It assumes that, in many cases, global cooperation should be based in law and should include enforceable rights and obligations. Such cooperation is almost inevitably connected with notions of global equity, and it also implies a belief in the desirability and feasibility of a future international legal order in which individuals as well as governments are subjects in their own right, as they are in domestic legal systems.

Some academics and officials say that the study of international organizations and international law is not yielding sufficient insights to help governments meet contemporary challenges, that these fields are not attracting a sufficient number of students, and that those now active in the fields have limited influence on public policy. There are two ways to explain this situation. It may be the result of external factors related to ideology, world events, or funding. Alternatively, the two fields may have internal problems related to staffing, organizational weakness, or an inability to address new problems with sufficient intellectual rigor. Both factors are probably at play, although the lack of international consensus suggests that external conditions in both the South and the North probably play a larger role. Nonetheless, there seems to be a clear need to bring new people and ideas into both fields and to promote interdisciplinary research.

Changes in international politics since World War II have also contributed to the decline in academic work on international organization and international law. Cooperation under Western hegemony in the early postwar period was easier to analyze than multilateral cooperation. Schemes for regional integration have different features in different regions, and global theories are little help in explaining them. Both fields have experienced growth and increasing specialization, making it harder to produce meaningful generalizations, and both now seem to be dominated by sub-fields, such as the environment, human rights, or international finance.

As the roles of governments and such non-state actors as large business corporations have become increasingly intertwined—particularly in the area of international economic law—it has become much harder to draw a dividing line between the fields of public international law, which governs relations between and the rights and duties of governments, and private international law, which determines, among other things, what legal system applies to international business transactions. This paper is predominantly concerned with subjects in the public domain.

Finally, as global organizations have come under political attack from various sides, analysis of their constitutions and formal structures seems less relevant than analysis of the political processes that govern them. This rapidly leads into the wider fields of international politics and economics.

Attention should also be directed to the changing position of national governments, particularly in their ability to commit themselves to long-term cooperation. Governments of industrialized democracies, which administer large welfare systems and are subject to pressure from various special-interest groups, have to take into account their constituencies' short-term interests. These interests can inhibit the governments' ability to take on long-term international commitments in such areas as trade relations or environmental protection. In fields like monetary relations, the predominance of multinational banks and corporations further complicates the picture. Research will have to pay more attention to the links between domestic and international politics and to the role of non-state actors on the international scene.

A similar need to broaden the scope of academic inquiry exists in the field of international law. According to the eminent scholar Oscar Schachter, limiting oneself to the general principles of classic public international law is like exploring a foreign country by driving only its highways: it doesn't tell you much about life in the towns and the villages. In his 1964 study *The Changing Structure of International Law*, Wolfgang Friedmann, one of Schachter's predecessors in the Hamilton Fish chair at Columbia University School of Law, made a crucial distinction: "In international law," Friedmann wrote, "it is today of both theoretical and practical importance to distinguish between the international law of 'coexistence,' governing essentially diplomatic inter-state relations, and the international law of co-operation, expressed in the growing structure of international organization and the pursuit of common human interest. From this follows the acknowledgment of the necessity of both universal and nonuniversal spheres of international law, depending on the degree of community of interests and purposes."*

Contrary to popular belief, international law does not exclusively, or even predominantly, serve the status quo. On the contrary, international law can be a powerful force for change, an important instrument for shaping more peaceful and more equitable relations between nations. One need only examine the evolution of the European Community to understand the potential of the international law of cooperation.

In sum, there is a need for new theories about international organizations and public international law. They can best be arrived at through interdisciplinary research that brings together lawyers and social scientists, theorists and practitioners, paying due attention to cultural and regional factors, to domestic politics, and to the role of non-state actors.

Lack of Training

Capacities to deal effectively with the challenges of international cooperation have become strained in industrialized and developing countries alike. A combination of research and teaching is necessary to further understanding of the complicated processes of decision making and negotiation that undergird efforts to secure international agreement. Because the intellectual requirements of both international organizations and public international law are daunting, it will require special efforts to attract the best minds to each field.

In developing countries, the particular need is for enhanced training in international organizations and law as a basis for strengthening participation in global institutions and improving the effectiveness of regional organizations. The Soviet Union and the countries of Central and Eastern Europe have training requirements of a very different nature, now that some of them have decided to integrate more closely into the international system. More than anything else, they require training in how to deal with market economies and pluralistic political systems.

*Wolfgang Friedmann, *The Changing Structure of International Law.* New York: Columbia University Press, 1964. Preface.

Many observers suggest that the United States also has a strong need to strengthen teaching and research in international organizations and public international law. Weaknesses here are attributed to the aging of a generation of outstanding teachers, the tenacity of unilateralist (go-it-alone) tendencies in American society, and the growing specialization in academic fields. Since few U.S. universities have evinced interest in addressing these weaknesses, special measures appear necessary to attract a new generation of scholars and practitioners to both fields.

A Foundation-supported conference on "Revitalizing the Study of International Organizations," held at the Fletcher School of Law and Diplomacy in October 1987, concluded that:

— writing on generic problems of international organizations has fallen off dramatically;

— there has been a significant decline in the number of relevant course offerings at major U.S. law and international relations schools;

— as a consequence, fewer students are developing an understanding of, and appreciation for, the work of international organizations;

— less and less professional legal training is available to those international officials, diplomats, government officials, and other public policy makers whose employment will put them in decision-making positions in or related to international organizations; and

— there has been insufficient commentary on multilateral issues by the academic community.

After broadly reviewing the status of scholarship on international organizations, the conference outlined an agenda for future teaching and research in this field. Recommendations covered possible research subjects, teaching methods and materials, and internships and fellowships to attract students to the field.

PREVIOUS FOUNDATION
GRANT MAKING

From the time the Ford Foundation became an international philanthropy in 1950, it has viewed the strengthening of international organizations as a priority concern. This Foundation interest follows a longstanding American philanthropic tradition. Before World War I, Andrew Carnegie donated the Peace Palace in The Hague. The Rockefeller family and its philanthropic institutions contributed heavily to the construction of both the Palais des Nations in Geneva in the 1920s and the United Nations in New York in the late 1940s. For its part, the Ford Foundation contributed to the construction of the United Nations Library and the U.N. International School, provided a large portion of the initial budgets of the U.N. Development Corporation, the Office of the U.N. High Commissioner for Refugees, and the U.N. Institute for Training and Research; it also supported the initial planning for the 1972 Stockholm Conference on the Human Environment, which gave rise to the U.N. Environment Programme. Altogether the Foundation has donated more than $26 million directly to the United Nations and its specialized agencies.

In the 1950s and 1960s the Foundation also gave large-scale support to private institutions concerned with international organizations and international law. It donated buildings and financed academic positions at several law schools in the United States and abroad. The focus then was not so much on public international law proper, but on what was called "international legal studies," which included comparative law, with a strong focus on international business transactions and a special emphasis on international and comparative tax law. Former deputy vice-president of the Foundation Francis X. Sutton, in a forthcoming book about the Foundation's international programs,* describes the philosophy behind this program and its evolution. Sutton says that the program reflected the great hope Americans had just after World War II for a world order based on the rule of law. Lawyers were seen as natural leaders of that order and the Foundation's investment in international legal studies was seen as a contribution to preparing such leaders, both in the United States and abroad. Even excluding grants for law and development overseas and for university support not

---

*Francis X. Sutton, "Leaders for a World Power—Especially Lawyers" (draft, April 21, 1989).

specifically directed to international legal studies, one may estimate that the Foundation gave at least $30 million to this loosely defined field.

The Foundation's support for the United Nations and for the international training of lawyers extended into the 1970s. By the late 1960s, however, the Foundation was scaling back its work in international organizations and law, reflecting growing disillusionment with the perceived inability of multilateral organizations and international law to fulfil the expectations that had been raised after 1945. It also reflected greater specialization within the broad field of international affairs and a focus on such topics as international economics and international security and arms control. With regard to law, attention to civil rights and international human rights gradually took the place of international legal studies as a focus of Foundation grant making

By the early 1980s, the so-called "crisis of multilateralism" was widely recognized. At that juncture, and in response to strong interest by its Board of Trustees, the Foundation decided to reaffirm its commitment to international institutions and multilateralism. A conference on international organizations sponsored by the Foundation in 1984 analyzed the nature of the crisis and ways to address it. Since then, the Foundation has made grants in response to opportunities as they arose. For example, support has gone to the International Peace Academy for policy analyses of international peace-keeping; to the American Society of International Law for research and conferences on the law of the sea and other global commons; and to the United Nations Association of the United States for public education. Initially, the Foundation supported a broad range of projects to assess existing multilateral institutions and to propose ways to improve their ability to respond to regional and global problems. The appointment in February 1986 of Brian Urquhart, former Under Secretary General of the United Nations for Special Political Affairs, as Scholar-in-Residence at the Foundation greatly enriched these activities.

Since 1985 Foundation funding for international organizations and law has increased steadily—from some $840,000 in 1985 to about $6.2 million in 1990.

A fter reviewing its work in consultation with outside specialists, the Foundation has decided to focus its work in international organizations and law on three broad objectives:

– Promoting research and policy analysis about the changing nature of multilateral cooperation. Special emphasis will be given to improving the integration of developing nations into the international system on terms acceptable to all.

– Strengthening the capacity of both scholars and practitioners, with initial emphases on teaching and research in public international law in the United States, and on teaching and research in both international organizations and public international law in developing countries, particularly in Africa.

– Promoting a better understanding of issues related to international organizations and public international law, particularly among the U.S. public.

Spending foreseen for these objectives for the 1990–91 biennium will amount to some $9 million.

Research and Policy Analysis

Because of the lack of consensus and understanding discussed earlier, there is a great need for research and policy analysis on multilateral cooperation. The concept of multilateralism has always needed explanation, given unilateralist reflexes and so-called *Realpolitik*. In order to demonstrate that multilateral cooperation can be a matter of enlightened self-interest, we must advance understanding of how international institutions actually work and how national interests can be pursued within and through them. Interdisciplinary research, policy analysis, and debate have much to contribute toward these ends.

The Foundation will continue to promote analyses of a wide range of issues related to international organizations and law. The following topics will be emphasized in the 1990–91 biennium:

- the United Nations system;
- international organizations and agreements generally;
- international peacekeeping and peacemaking;
- sustainable development and management of the global commons; and
- institutional and legal aspects of regional integration and cooperation.

In all these areas, special attention will be paid to identifying the stake that developing countries have in strengthening international organizations and international legal arrangements, and to examining the conditions under which developing countries can be better integrated into the international system.

The United Nations System

The United Nations system, with its virtually universal membership, remains a natural focus for any inquiry into the changing role of international organizations. The system suffers from obvious weaknesses that must be carefully analyzed, and various U.N. activities should be compared with those of other international organizations. In other words, the focus of research and discussion should be the functions to be performed by international institutions, not simply on the U.N. itself.

The United Nations Association of the United States of America (UNA–USA) is the principal U.S. public policy organization concerned with the U.N. Although it has for many years devoted some of its resources to activities only tangentially related to the U.N., UNA–USA has lately begun to undertake critical policy analysis and debate about the U.N. system. A Foundation grant to UNA–USA for a study of management and decision making at the United Nations resulted in the report, *A Successor Vision: The United Nations of Tomorrow.** Although few of its recommendations have found their way into the political process, they remain available for action by member states. Another grant supported a bilateral dialogue between the UNA–USA and the UNA–USSR on how both superpowers can make better use of various U.N. instruments, such as peacekeeping, the good offices of the Secretary General, and the International Court of Justice. Also, a grant to UNA–USA supported an international panel on the mission of the United Nations Educational, Scientific and Cultural Organization (UNESCO) as well as a study of conditions necessary for the United States to rejoin UNESCO. Early in 1990,

---

*Peter Fromuth, ed., *A Successor Vision: The United Nations of Tomorrow.* New York: United Nations Association of the United States of America, 1988.

15

a grant of $1.2 million was made to UNA–USA to help it increase its membership and strengthen its chapters; further its links with the academic community; and enhance its Washington office and services to the media.

The American Society of International Law (ASIL), long supported by the Foundation, is conducting a study of the United Nations' contribution to the international legal order. The study coincides with a time when nations from East and West and North and South are showing increased interest in international dispute settlement. Other Foundation-supported ASIL studies deal with subjects that are under the jurisdiction of the International Court of Justice.

In 1988 the Foundation helped establish the Academic Council on the U.N. System (ACUNS), which consists of a group of social scientists and legal scholars from the United States, Canada, and Mexico who specialize in studies of international organizations. In 1989 the Foundation gave ACUNS general support for a long-term program aimed at strengthening teaching and research in the field. To that end, ACUNS will develop specialized research on organizations, issues, and cases. The Foundation will encourage close cooperation between UNA–USA, ASIL, and ACUNS, and, in particular, will assist ASIL and ACUNS in organizing summer workshops on international organizations for young social scientists and public international law scholars.

Since Brian Urquhart came to the Foundation as Scholar-in-Residence after his retirement from the United Nations in February 1986, he has carried out a number of in-house projects. The most ambitious deals with the leadership of the U.N. system in the 1990s, which focuses on the selection and appointment of the U.N. Secretary General, the heads of the specialized agencies, and various other top U.N. officials. The resulting study, entitled "A World in Need of Leadership: Tomorrow's United Nations," will be published in various languages in September 1990, under the joint auspices of the Ford Foundation and the Dag Hammarskjöld Foundation in Uppsala, Sweden.

Since a large project undertaken by the Carnegie Endowment in the early 1950s, no systematic study has been made of the policies of various nations toward the United Nations. To help fill this gap, the Foundation granted funds to the University of Ottawa for an international project involving analysis of the policies of eighteen nations toward the United Nations. The project culminated in a conference in Ottawa in January 1990.

Other work along these lines will be encouraged.

General Aspects of International Organizations

Several grants have been made on this broad subject since 1985. For example, the Foundation supported two seminars of social scientists from Massachusetts and California. The first group, led by Prof. Robert Keohane of Harvard University's Department of Government, is, among other things, analyzing why nations comply with international obligations even when it does not seem to serve their immediate interests. The West Coast group, coordinated by Prof. John Gerard Ruggie of the University of California, San Diego, is studying the nature of multilateralism. Both groups include promising younger scholars. In addition, a grant to Dartmouth College is supporting a program on international cooperation in the Arctic region, and a grant was made to Princeton University for a study, directed by Prof. Leon Gordenker, of why and how international cooperation has emerged in response to AIDS.

The Foundation also intends to encourage research on the relation between international organizations and problems addressed by international economists, environmental specialists, and security and arms control specialists. Studies of these complicated questions will require close cooperation among a wide variety of disciplines, from political science and law to economics and history.

International Peacekeeping and Peacemaking

Given its intergovernmental context and the fairly straightforward nature of the functions it performs, peacekeeping is a task that capitalizes on the strength of the U.N. With the recent improvement of relations between the two superpowers, and the interest of the Soviet leadership in limiting direct involvement in regional conflicts, continued development of peacekeeping techniques seems possible. Conferences on Cambodia and the U.N. and on a system for U.N. peacemaking and peacekeeping, which were convened by Brian Urquhart at the Ford Foundation, focused on the increasingly salient issue of involving peacekeeping forces in domestic conflicts and on ways to go beyond the present ad hoc approach in managing and financing U.N. peacemaking and peacekeeping.

Over the past few years, the Foundation has made several grants to the International Peace Academy (IPA) in New York. A recent grant is supporting IPA's Special Research Program on Peacekeeping, which is being carried out in collaboration with the Norwegian Institute of International Affairs—also a recipient of several Foundation grants on peacekeeping—and with the Centre for International and Strategic Studies at York University in Canada. A second grant to IPA is supporting training seminars and workshops on regional peacekeeping and conflict resolution in developing countries.

In the summer of 1990, grants for work on aspects of peacekeeping were awarded to the Canadian Centre for Arms Control and Disarmament, the Norwegian Institute of International Affairs, and the Stimson Center in Washington, D.C. The grants were awarded in an international research competition that focused on global and regional approaches to conventional arms control and international peacekeeping. The links between these subjects and regional conflict resolution are obvious. If alternative mechanisms for providing regional security—for example, preventive diplomacy, outside guarantees, demilitarized zones—could be put in place, the need for expensive armaments programs would be diminished. This argues for close coordination of grant making in the fields of international security and arms control and international peacekeeping. Work on regional conflict resolution has been assisted by a number of grants, one of which supports the activities of the United Nations Regional Centre for Peace and Disarmament in Africa in Lomé, Togo. While recognizing that support for United Nations peacemaking and peacekeeping is the responsibility of its member states, the Foundation has recently contributed to a newly established United Nations trust fund, which will support peacemaking activities of the Secretary General and his representatives and which will be used at his sole discretion.

The Foundation intends to explore ways to broaden its support for peacekeeping to include preventive diplomacy by the U.N. Secretary General as well as various early-warning and monitoring systems by the U.N. Secretariat. Of great importance are the links between peacekeeping and public international law. To support such links, a grant went to the American Society of International Law for work with Soviet counterparts on the use of force and the peaceful settlement of disputes.

Sustainable Development and Management of the Global Commons

The management of shared resources like rivers and oceans has historically proven to be both a source of conflict and a challenge for cooperation in order to maximize common interests. Various bilateral and multilateral agencies established for the joint management of international river basins are excellent examples of international cooperation and set precedents for more ambitious arrangements. The 1982 United Nations Convention on the Law of the Sea remains the most far-reaching attempt by the world's nations to arrive at agreement on regulating conflicting uses of a shared resource. The oceans are the global commons par excellence, although others are now presenting themselves with increasing urgency, for example, the environment, Antarctica, and outer space.

These issues cut across three areas of Foundation interest: resources and the environment; international economics; and the institutional and legal dimensions of sustainable development and global management. Future grants will continue to support projects to advance sustainable development and the management of global commons.

For the immediate future, the Foundation's work on international riverways will be somewhat diminished, largely in order to free resources for newer problems of worldwide as opposed to regional concern.

In 1989 a supplementary grant was made to the Council on Ocean Law, which has done excellent work related to the Law of the Sea Treaty. A team of scholars, assembled by the American Society of International Law and partially supported by the Foundation, is presently examining the settlement of maritime boundary disputes between coastal states in various parts of the world. The aim is to determine whether particular methods used to resolve those disputes could be applied to the resolution of remaining maritime boundary conflicts. The project is investigating whether there are patterns that might be taken as evidence of rules of customary international law.

A grant to the Woods Hole Oceanographic Institution is supporting an international planning group on fishery statistics. It is addressing problems in the current system of statistical reporting, which are hampering management of the fishery resources of the global commons. Through a grant to the International Ocean Institute on Malta, the Foundation is supporting a study of the possibility of protecting the Mediterranean marine environment by means of an international tourist tax earmarked for the Trust Fund of the United Nations Environment Programme.

Our Common Future, the report of the World Commission on Environment and Development,* which was partially supported by the Foundation, focused world attention on a number of global environmental changes as well as on the increasing dangers, particularly in certain parts of the developing world, of the destruction of ecological support systems that are vital for future economic development. Other Foundation grants in this field include one to the World Resources Institute for an interdisciplinary panel on the "greenhouse" effect and global climate change. A planning grant to the World Federation of United Nations Associations has enabled an international team led by Maurice Strong to organize a project on global security and multilateralism. It is focusing on "outer boundaries," such as those related to environmental and resource constraints that cannot be transgressed without major risks for the future of the globe.

As noted, there is a great need for innovative institutional, legal, and

*The World Commission on Environment and Development, *Our Common Future*. Oxford/New York: Oxford University Press, 1987.

economic approaches in this area. They should provide developing countries with greater incentives to cooperate—for example, by paying compensation for opportunities forgone by the adoption of measures to protect the global environment. Some have proposed transforming the present U.N. Trusteeship Council into an international trust administering global resources and providing trustees with compensation, perhaps by mandatory pro-rata assessment of all member states.

The Foundation is presently exploring ways to support the participation of developing-country governments and nongovernmental organizations in preparations for the 1992 U.N. Conference on Environment and Development in Brazil. The Foundation also hopes to strengthen capacities in developing countries to deal with policy issues related to the global environment. A grant to the Centre for International Environmental Law in London has enabled a group of American and British legal scholars to research the legal ramifications of global warming and to help geographically vulnerable developing states participate more fully in international negotiations on the effects of global warming.

Recently, Brian Urquhart convened a meeting at the Foundation involving representatives from U.N. missions, high U.N. officials, and some independent experts to discuss the ability of the United Nations system to deal with issues of the environment and development.

Regional Integration and Cooperation

As the previous analysis suggests, regional integration and cooperation may become more common in the years to come. The Foundation has supported efforts at regional integration in various developing areas. For example, grants have gone to the Preferential Trade Area for Eastern and Southern African States, to the Southern Africa Development Coordination Conference, to the Arab Thought Forum in Amman, which is financing research on regional cooperation in the Arab region, and to Duke University in support of the International Commission for Central American Recovery and Development.

The Foundation is also supporting the new European Community Studies Association, which facilitates networking among U.S. scholars studying the evolving roles of the European Community. Part of the Foundation's grant will support a workshop on relations among the European Community, the United States, and the developing world in the 1990s. A grant to the Hague Academy of International Law supported an international workshop on possible future dispute-settlement mechanisms between European nations pertaining to territorial as well as non-territorial disputes, including those over the environment and human rights. A grant to the University of Chicago School of Law is supporting a conference on the legal restructuring of the European Community as well as publication of conference papers.

Capacity Building

The Foundation's focus is on public international law, rather than comparative or private international law, on the study of international organizations, and, wherever possible, cooperation with social scientists. In the United States, the Foundation will concentrate on helping to produce a new generation of broadly trained public international lawyers. In the developing countries, grants will focus on assisting scholars and practitioners in international organizations and law, particularly in Africa.

Public international lawyers have a crucial role to play in strengthening multilateralism, which is, after all, cast in a framework of treaty obligations and pursued through various legal mechanisms. The field of public international law faces particular problems in the United States, however. Foundation discussions with law school deans and professors revealed that large numbers of students enter law school with strong interest in international issues and the role of international organizations in managing tensions and problems between nations. Yet, as their studies proceed, students obtain very little exposure to public international law, either through course work, faculty advice and assistance, or employment opportunities. As a result, their early interest dims and is ultimately displaced by the study of other subjects.

A number of leading law schools have no permanent international law scholar on the faculty. Faculty vacancies in the field are not filled. Some claim that there is a shortage of excellent young teachers of public international law because of years of neglect of the field. In many cases, the general introductory course on public international law is offered only occasionally by part-time or visiting scholars from other schools or by faculty members with other primary interests. Some argue that this condition reflects the general disillusionment with international cooperation in the United States and that the situation can only be turned around by a change in overall public perceptions. However, they also note that recent developments, like the growing importance of international legal standards in the environment and human rights fields, are beginning to stimulate new interest among students and faculty.

The main problem, therefore, concerns the teaching of public international law, primarily in law schools, but also in international affairs schools and social science departments, which also have neglected the subject in recent years. There are three major, interrelated needs: encouraging schools to pay more attention to public international law, providing support to existing scholars, and attracting young lawyers to the field. Building a new generation of public international law professors to succeed the high-calibre postwar generation of legal scholars will be difficult, however, because of the many lucrative alternative options available to the best U.S. law school graduates.

The Foundation is currently addressing the question of how to attract bright graduates to the teaching of public international law. We believe interest in the field can be stimulated initially by expanding and enriching course offerings, establishing attractive fellowships for future law professors, creating internships and summer jobs, and supporting research. We also believe that these mechanisms will indirectly stimulate the interest of larger numbers of students over the longer term. The Foundation's recent experiences in human rights law seem to confirm this view.

In Spring 1990 grants totaling $1.6 million were made to six major U.S. law schools—at Columbia, Georgetown, Harvard, New York, and Yale universities, and the University of Michigan—as well as to the Fletcher School of Law and Diplomacy. All have a strong record in producing excellent teachers of law. These grants are mainly supporting fellowship and internship programs for J.D. as well as graduate degree candidates. They also cover costs of colloquia, teaching seminars, and various outreach activities. It is envisaged that in the fall of 1990 a second set of grants for a comparable amount will be recommended for other law schools and international affairs schools across the United States. Over the past two years, Foundation staff have visited or been in touch with some forty such institutions.

In addition to supporting law-school fellowships in public international law, grants will also contribute to the expansion of overall course offerings in international organizations and public international law, in particular by improving curricular materials for introductory courses. Support may also go to measures to give U.S. students more information about professional opportunities for public international lawyers. Finally, summer internships will be supported. For example, a grant to the State University of New York at Buffalo enabled Virginia Leary, Professor of International Law, to develop a summer internship program at international organizations in Geneva. Another grant enabled the Ralph Bunche Institute of the City University of New York to expand educational opportunities for minority students in international organizations. Other such programs will be explored.

In all these activities, special attention will be paid to encouraging minorities and women to study public international law, mainly by assisting institutions that have a proven ability to attract them and by developing rosters of female and minority scholars and consultants. Overall, the Foundation hopes to help re-create law-school centers of excellence in public international law, much as it did in international legal studies in the 1950s and 1960s at Harvard, Michigan, Yale, and other universities.

Related activities will strive to raise the status of the field generally. The American Society of International Law (ASIL) can play an important role in this regard. Through its sponsorship of the prestigious annual Jessup Competition, a moot court for public international law, its annual meetings, and publication of the *American Journal of International Law,* ASIL is already doing important work in attracting students and young scholars to public international law.

The Foundation will continue to encourage ASIL's efforts to identify younger scholars for leadership in ASIL's panels and research projects. For example, young scholars are directing ASIL's Maritime Boundary Project, mentioned earlier, as well as its Program of U.S.–Soviet Research in International Law, which is conducted in cooperation with the Institute of State and Law of the Academy of Sciences of the USSR and the Soviet Association of International Law. The Foundation is currently supporting ASIL's "Survey of Academic International Law in North America and Abroad." Both its steering committee and international advisory committee include promising new U.S. scholars.

Although the Foundation has decided to focus initially on the field of public international law, its support of the Academic Council on the United Nations System (ACUNS) should help improve the quality of teaching and research on the United Nations and other international organizations in social science faculties as well as in law schools. ACUNS' Standing Committee on Teaching is paying particular attention to improving teaching materials. Another proposed activity is to promote contacts between U.N. officials and university faculty, which may help lower barriers between the somewhat insular world of the U.N. and academics and others interested in international organizations. As mentioned earlier, the Foundation will explore the possibility of supporting summer workshops on international organizations for young scholars in the social sciences, international relations, and international law. Attention will also be given to exchanges between various faculties.

The second component of capacity building concerns developing countries. Public international law would be too narrow a focus here, considering the limited capacities of most developing countries to play active roles in international organizations. This is particularly true of their participation in economic institutions, such as the General Agreement on Tariffs and Trade (GATT) and the International Monetary Fund. For many years, developing countries have concentrated their multilateral diplomacy in such forums as the U.N. General Assembly and the United Nations Conference on Trade and Development, which enabled them to air their grievances but rarely produced negotiations that improved actual conditions in their countries.

A grant to the International Development Law Institute in Rome is supporting the institute's programs for mid-career legal advisors in developing countries whose job responsibilities include management of debts and financial assets.

Besides supporting training in international organizations and public international law in developing countries, the Foundation will encourage institutions in industrialized countries—such as U.S. law schools—to contribute to the development of specialized expertise in developing countries. One such activity, for example, might be research on topics of particular interest to developing countries, such as international environmental law. Other examples include strengthening capacities in developing countries in the peaceful settlement of disputes, in management of the global commons, and in dealing with and learning from the European Community. The Foundation also hopes to promote contacts between selected academic centers in the developing world, particularly in Africa, and U.S. and European centers of excellence in public international law, through support for visiting scholars and participation in research and training programs.

Too little attention has been given to the way people from various cultures participate in international organizations and international legal arrangements. For example, not much is known about how such concepts as human rights or sustainable development are absorbed in developing countries. The Foundation is exploring the possibility of advancing understanding of such subjects.

Public Education

Among the U.S. public at large, there is increasing interest in certain global issues, particularly the environment. At the same time, attitudes toward the U.N. seem to vary from moderate approval to outright skepticism. And yet there are indications that important parts of the American public are interested in multilateral approaches to important world problems.

In a sense, the jury is still out on the question of whether the U.N. system will be able to meet the challenges posed by new global issues. Hence, public education faces several problems. Explaining the intrinsic value of multilateralism is complicated; the U.N. may not be able to prove itself a credible participant in some of the most crucial issues of the future; and focusing on a few topical issues may not be enough to meet the challenges of global coexistence.

The experience of the United Nations Association of the United States of America reflects many of these problems. Promoting the U.N. has not been a very popular task in recent years, and may not be in the future. Nevertheless, emerging global issues offer a means of raising UNA's profile and should be a spur to rejuvenating local chapters. Part of the $1.2 million grant to UNA–USA mentioned earlier has been earmarked for this purpose. Given the current fragmentation within the nongovernmental community regarding international organizations and law, there seems room for some networking in which UNA–USA could play a useful role.

In late 1989 the Foundation supported the National Conference on the United States and the United Nations, convened by UNA–USA's Council of Organizations in Washington D.C. This was the first comprehensive national assembly of U.S. citizens in recent years to consider the role that the United States should play in the United Nations, its specialized agencies, and associated financial institutions.

A grant in 1989 to the Southern Center for International Studies in Atlanta supported a televised discussion on "The U.N.: What's In It for the U.S.?" among former U.S. Permanent Representatives to the U.N. The debate was edited into an hourlong television program that was broadcast nationwide on National Public Television in June 1989 and, with additional interviews with Brian Urquhart, made into educational videotapes. Support has also been given to National Public Radio for increased coverage of international organizations, particularly the U.N. A small grant was made for the production of demonstration materials for a video-based educational program aimed at high school students. Called "World Issues and the United Nations," it was produced by the Friends of the United Nations in cooperation with the National Education Association and the National Council for the Social Studies.

The 1989–90 General Assembly of the United Nations approved a resolution, prepared by members of the Non-Aligned Movement in The Hague, proposing to declare a Decade of International Law leading up to the centennial of the 1899 Peace Conference in The Hague. One of the objectives would be to examine the compulsory jurisdiction of the International Court of Justice (ICJ). The Foundation may support various NGO projects dealing with this subject and with the role of the ICJ generally.

A grant to Parliamentarians Global Action for Disarmament, Development and World Reform is supporting program activities aimed at improving understanding among members of parliaments around the world about international peacekeeping and public international law and their potential for improving global welfare. Another recent grant has enabled the Foundation Emmes, in cooperation with the Business Council for the United Nations, to organize a series of evening conferences in the United States Capitol Building. At each conference members of the U.S. Congress, high United Nations officials, and representatives of the business community will review one particular U.N. agency, program, or activity, assess its effectiveness, and discuss how the United States and the United Nations might work together more effectively. A grant to the American Society of International Law is supporting ten one-day conferences, to be held in various parts of the United States, on aspects of public international law of concern to particular regions. The meetings will be organized by local experts and involve academics, policy makers, journalists, and members of the public from the respective regions.

The Foundation is also exploring other means of promoting public awareness of issues related to international organizations and public international law and of expanding interest in them through activities other than grant making. Some research policy institutes that are longstanding Foundation grantees might be persuaded to include consideration of them as part of their regular programs. Moreover, given the Foundation's own funding constraints, it would be desirable if other foundations also decided to support programs in international organizations and law. To encourage such interest, the Foundation convened a one-day meeting in the fall of 1989 to discuss the needs of both fields with representatives from other foundations, think-tanks, and foreign-policy institutes. Similar activities may be organized in the future.